WHAT IS A METAPH

GW00455886

Metaphors are a POETIC DEVICE: Figurative language comparing two **unlike things.** Stating that one "IS" the other.

Metaphors **ARE** magic tricks that give words more meaning.
Example: Life **IS** pure poetry.

WHY MAKE METAPHORS?

Metaphors can communicate more depth and breadth than literal statements. The truths contained in metaphorical expressions are deeper, more nuanced, and more memorable to your reader. Metaphors provide interesting jumping- off-points for any type of writing and help break through writer's block.

WHERE ARE METAPHORS USED?

Metaphors are used in all forms of writing: poems, narratives, novels, essays, song lyrics, dialogue, speeches, emails, or anywhere you want your writing to stand-out and speak clearer than "literal" words. Metaphors will make you an **unforgettable** writer by helping you to say what you really mean.

WHO USES METAPHORS?

Authors and poets, advertisers, hit-song writers, world leaders, historians, and influencers use metaphors to communicate.

You probably use metaphors all the time.
Surely, you've said something like...

"Poetry is a huge drag, " or "Dude, that poem was a sick ride!"

WHAT'S IN A METAPHOR?

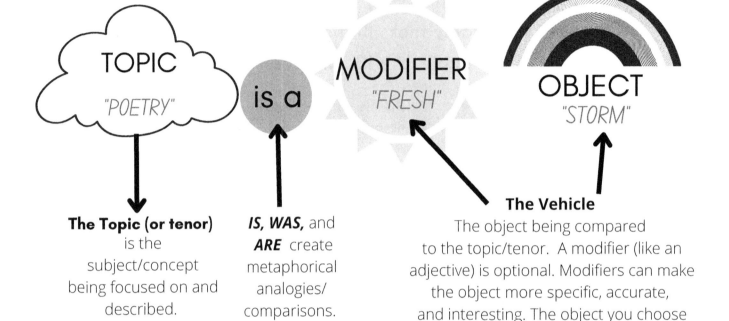

TOPIC
"POETRY"

is a

MODIFIER
"FRESH"

OBJECT
"STORM"

The Topic (or tenor) is the subject/concept being focused on and described.

IS, WAS, and **ARE** create metaphorical analogies/ comparisons.

The Vehicle
The object being compared to the topic/tenor. A modifier (like an adjective) is optional. Modifiers can make the object more specific, accurate, and interesting. The object you choose should **not** have any **literal** connection to the topic. Example: "Candy is a sweet treat." is too literal.

POETRY IS A FRESH STORM.

Poetry isn't literally a storm. However, reading and writing poetry can feel like the words are falling on your brain like torrential rain. The adjective **"fresh"** is defined as: just made or brand new. A poem written 100 years ago can feel as relevant and "fresh" as if it had been written today. The form or order may change. For example: A fresh storm of poetry arrived today.

MAKE YOUR OWN METAPHORS

IN THIS BOOK, YOU CAN CREATE UNIQUE METAPHORS IN TWO WAYS.

CONNECT THE DOTS or LET THE CARDS DECIDE
then...
EXPLAIN, GIVE EXAMPLES, AND ELABORATE on the metaphors you make.
Turn your metaphors into poems, dialogue, rap lyrics, catchy hooks, unforgettable concluding statements, or an inspiring call to action.

CONNECT
THE
DOTS

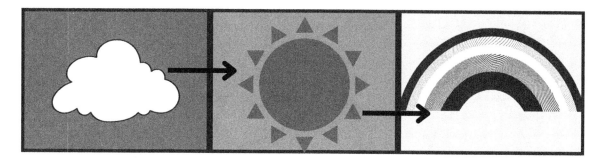

1. **Connect the dots:** draw lines to connect a topic + a modifier + an object = a metaphor.

2. **Write** your combinations and ideas in the spaces provided.

3. **Explain, give examples and elaborate** on the metaphors you create.

4. **Create:** Turn your metaphors into poems, dialogue, rap lyrics, catchy hooks, unforgettable concluding statements, or an inspiring calls to action.

EXAMPLE
METAPHOR MAKER

Connect the dots to combine: a topic, a modifier and an object.
Make as many unique and meaningful combinations as you can.

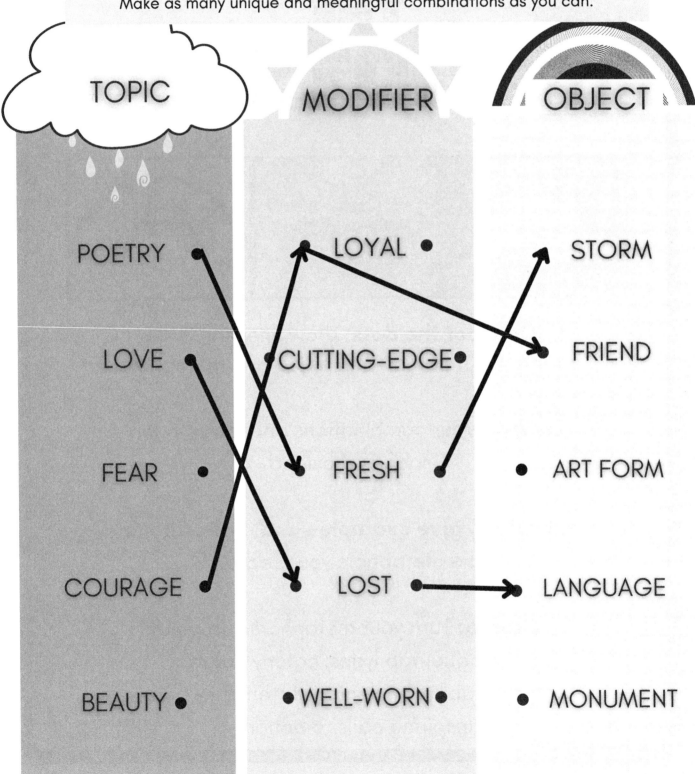

TOPIC

MODIFIER

OBJECT

POETRY

LOYAL

STORM

LOVE

CUTTING-EDGE

FRIEND

FEAR

FRESH

ART FORM

COURAGE

LOST

LANGUAGE

BEAUTY

WELL-WORN

MONUMENT

EXAMPLE
METAPHOR MAKER

TOPIC

Poetry

is a
are

MODIFIER

fresh

OBJECT

storm

POETRY IS A FRESH STORM

LOVE IS A LOST LANGUAGE

COURAGE IS A LOYAL FRIEND.

BEAUTY IS A WELL-WORN ART FORM

Explanation:

A torrent of words can rain
down without a moment's notice,
to spoil picnics and flood journals.

Examples:

Clear skies can fill with cotton candy clouds,
deafening thunder claps,
and blinding lightning slaps.

Elaboration:

Prepare to turn that bright-yellow
umbrella-frown upside-down.
Capture every pitter-patter of poetry
and save them for a sunny day.

METAPHOR MAKER

Connect the dots to combine: a topic, a modifier and an object.
Make as many unique and meaningful combinations as you can.

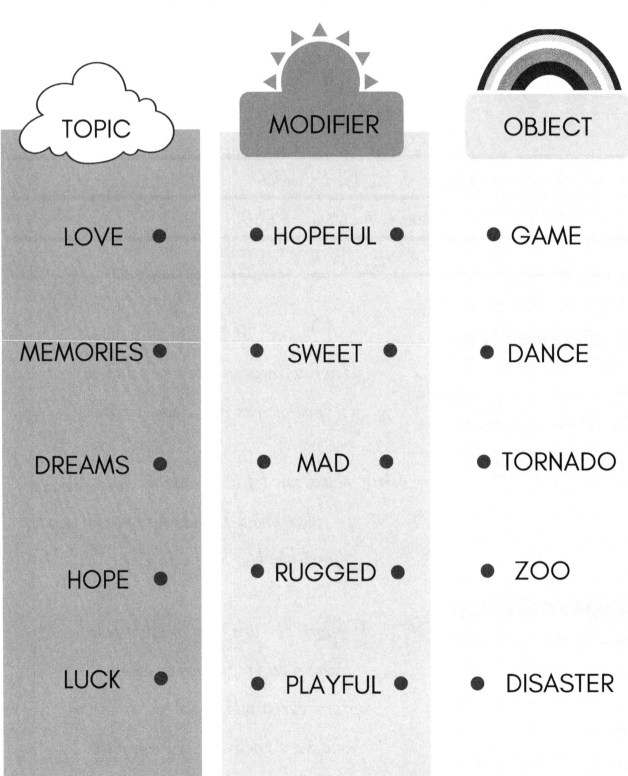

TOPIC	MODIFIER	OBJECT
LOVE	HOPEFUL	GAME
MEMORIES	SWEET	DANCE
DREAMS	MAD	TORNADO
HOPE	RUGGED	ZOO
LUCK	PLAYFUL	DISASTER

METAPHOR MAKER

 TOPIC   is a / are    MODIFIER    OBJECT

_____

_____

_____

Explanation:

Examples:

Elaboration:

METAPHOR MAKER

Connect the dots to combine: a topic, a modifier and an object.
Make as many unique and meaningful combinations as you can.

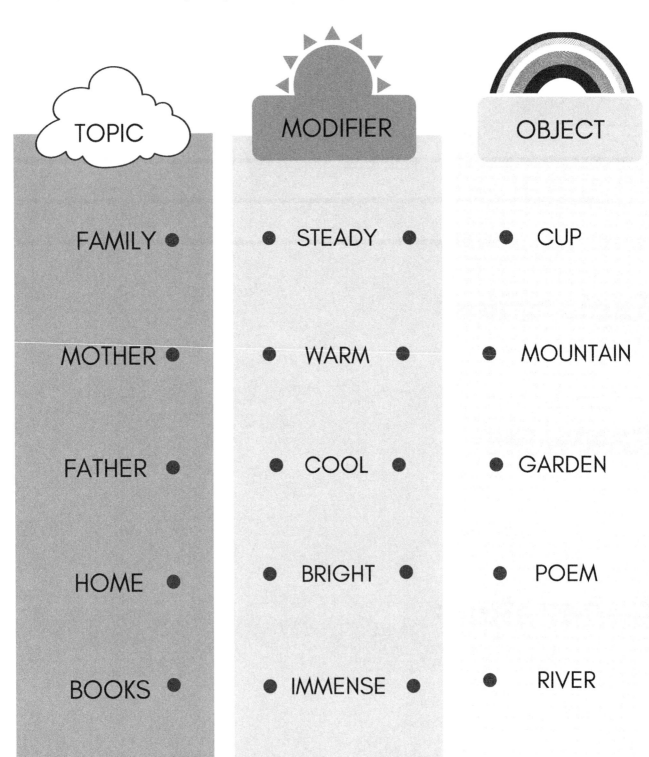

TOPIC	MODIFIER	OBJECT
FAMILY	STEADY	CUP
MOTHER	WARM	MOUNTAIN
FATHER	COOL	GARDEN
HOME	BRIGHT	POEM
BOOKS	IMMENSE	RIVER

METAPHOR MAKER

 TOPIC

is a / are

 MODIFIER

 OBJECT

_____

_____

_____

Explanation:

Examples:

Elaboration:

METAPHOR MAKER

Connect the dots to combine: a topic, a modifier and an object.
Make as many unique and meaningful combinations as you can.

TOPIC	MODIFIER	OBJECT
SCHOOL	DISTANT	THUNDER
MATH	FALLING	MOUNTAIN
TEACHER	EAGER	PENCIL
HOMEWORK	LOST	LANGUAGE
HISTORY	FOREIGN	CIRCUS

METAPHOR MAKER

 TOPIC

is a
are

 MODIFIER

 OBJECT

_____

_____

_____

Explanation:

Examples:

Elaboration:

METAPHOR MAKER

Connect the dots to combine: a topic, a modifier and an object.
Make as many unique and meaningful combinations as you can.

 **TOPIC**

 **MODIFIER**

 **OBJECT**

TOPIC	MODIFIER	OBJECT
SOCCER	TANGLED	RIDE
FOOTBALL	MIGHTY	LANGUAGE
TENNIS	LOUD	BEAST
BASEBALL	RUGGED	BATTLE
HOCKEY	FROZEN	EARTHQUAKE

METAPHOR MAKER

 TOPIC

is a
———
are

 MODIFIER

 OBJECT

_____

_____

_____

Explanation:

Examples:

Elaboration:

METAPHOR MAKER

Connect the dots to combine: a topic, a modifier and an object.
Make as many unique and meaningful combinations as you can.

 **TOPIC**

 **MODIFIER**

 **OBJECT**

TOPIC	MODIFIER	OBJECT
DOG	CUDDLY	HUG
CAT	FLUFFY	PARTY
RABBIT	MIDNIGHT	GHOST
HORSE	DROOLING	PILLOW
UNICORN	VELVET	MARSHMALLOW

METAPHOR MAKER

 TOPIC

is a
___
are

 MODIFIER

 OBJECT

_____

_____

_____

Explanation:

Examples:

Elaboration:

METAPHOR MAKER

Connect the dots to combine: a topic, a modifier and an object.
Make as many unique and meaningful combinations as you can.

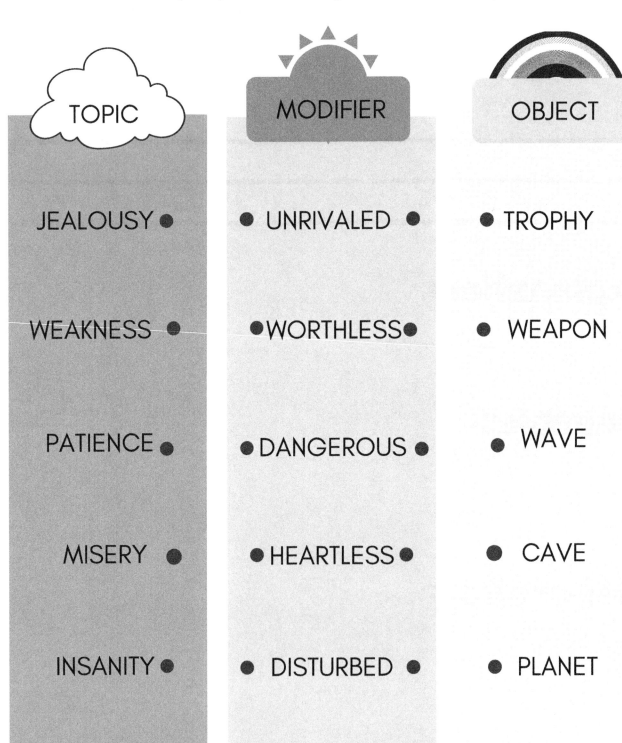

TOPIC	MODIFIER	OBJECT
JEALOUSY	UNRIVALED	TROPHY
WEAKNESS	WORTHLESS	WEAPON
PATIENCE	DANGEROUS	WAVE
MISERY	HEARTLESS	CAVE
INSANITY	DISTURBED	PLANET

METAPHOR MAKER

 TOPIC | is a / are |  MODIFIER |  OBJECT

Explanation:

Examples:

Elaboration:

METAPHOR MAKER

Connect the dots to combine: a topic, a modifier and an object.
Make as many unique and meaningful combinations as you can.

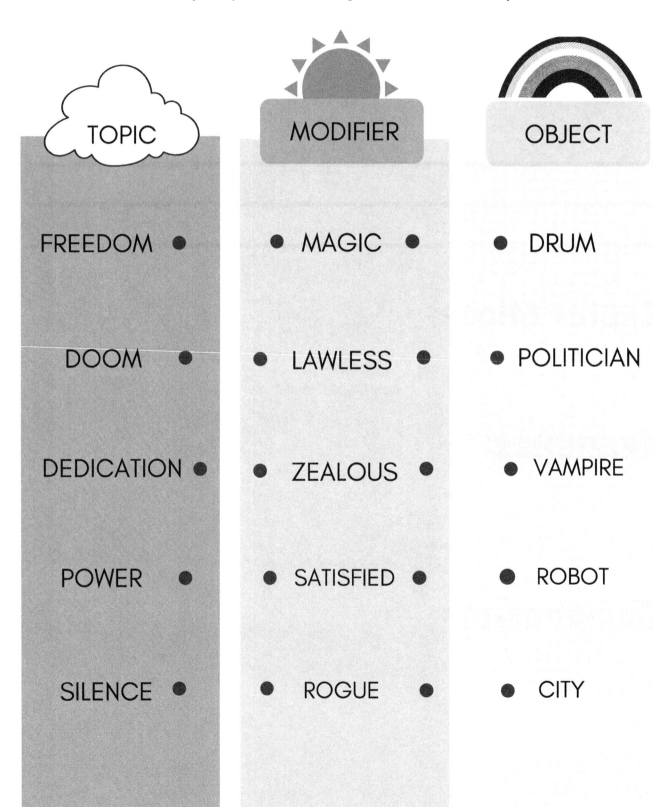

TOPIC	MODIFIER	OBJECT
FREEDOM	MAGIC	DRUM
DOOM	LAWLESS	POLITICIAN
DEDICATION	ZEALOUS	VAMPIRE
POWER	SATISFIED	ROBOT
SILENCE	ROGUE	CITY

METAPHOR MAKER

 TOPIC | is a / are |  MODIFIER |  OBJECT

_____

_____

_____

Explanation:

Examples:

Elaboration:

METAPHOR MAKER

Connect the dots to combine: a topic, a modifier and an object.
Make as many unique and meaningful combinations as you can.

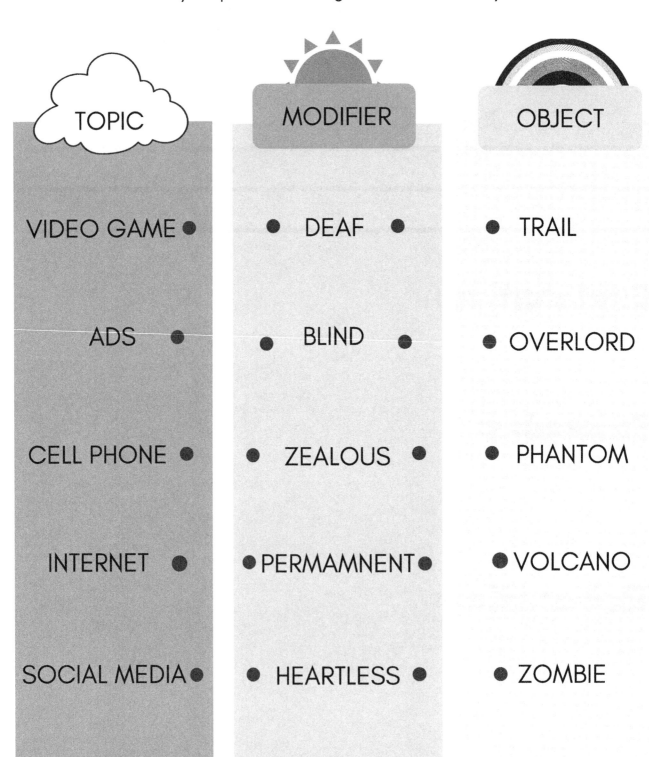

TOPIC	MODIFIER	OBJECT
VIDEO GAME	DEAF	TRAIL
ADS	BLIND	OVERLORD
CELL PHONE	ZEALOUS	PHANTOM
INTERNET	PERMAMNENT	VOLCANO
SOCIAL MEDIA	HEARTLESS	ZOMBIE

METAPHOR MAKER

 TOPIC   is a / are    MODIFIER    OBJECT

_____

_____

_____

Explanation:

Examples:

Elaboration:

METAPHOR MAKER

TOPIC

- SLEEP
- DREAMS
- NIGHTMARES
- DAY DREAMS
- WAKING UP

MODIFIER

- HEARTLESS
- LAME
- FRIGHTENING
- WILLFUL
- SLOBBERING

OBJECT

- MEDICINE
- MUSIC
- PRAYER
- PROMISE
- QUIZ

METAPHOR MAKER

 **TOPIC** _____ is a / are  MODIFIER  OBJECT

_____

_____

_____

Explanation:

Examples:

Elaboration:

METAPHOR MAKER

Connect the dots to combine: a topic, a modifier and an object.
Make as many unique and meaningful combinations as you can.

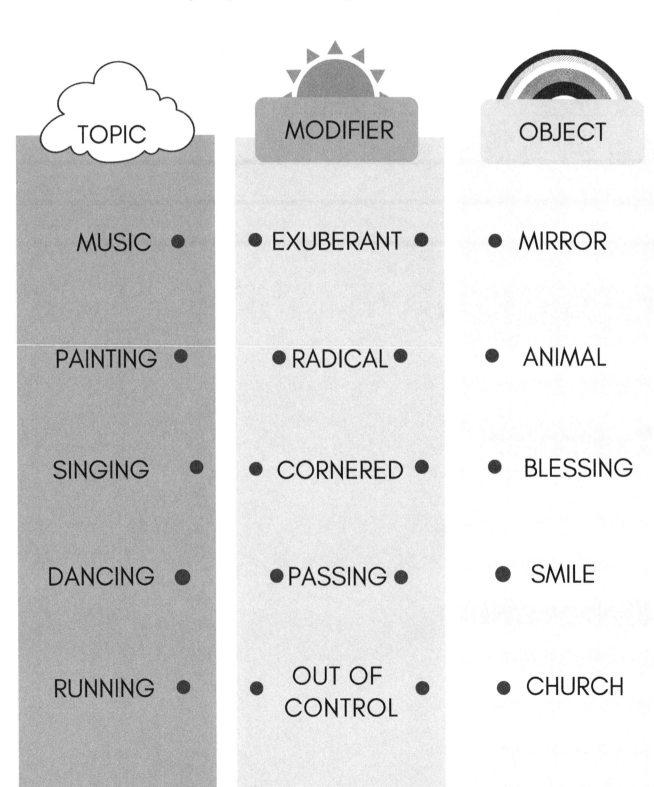

TOPIC	MODIFIER	OBJECT
MUSIC	EXUBERANT	MIRROR
PAINTING	RADICAL	ANIMAL
SINGING	CORNERED	BLESSING
DANCING	PASSING	SMILE
RUNNING	OUT OF CONTROL	CHURCH

METAPHOR MAKER

 **TOPIC** is a / are  MODIFIER  OBJECT

_____

_____

_____

Explanation:

Examples:

Elaboration:

METAPHOR MAKER

Connect the dots to combine: a topic, a modifier and an object.
Make as many unique and meaningful combinations as you can.

TOPIC	MODIFIER	OBJECT
LAUGHTER	LEAKY	HANDSHAKE
LIES	SINKING	TEAPOT
ALIBIS	CRACKED	SHIP
IDOLS	SLIPPERY	BATHTUB
DARES	CLOSING	TEMPLE

METAPHOR MAKER

TOPIC

is a
are

MODIFIER

OBJECT

_____

_____

_____

Explanation:

Examples:

Elaboration:

METAPHOR MAKER

Connect the dots to combine: a topic, a modifier and an object.
Make as many unique and meaningful combinations as you can.

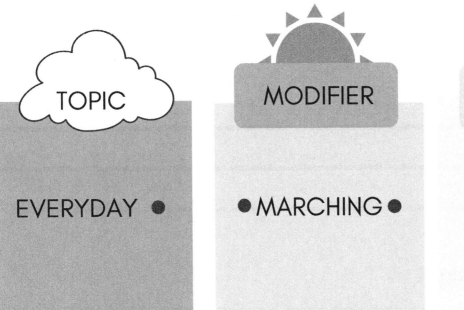

TOPIC	MODIFIER	OBJECT
EVERYDAY ●	● MARCHING ●	● SEASHORE
YESTERDAY ●	● CRAWLING ●	● SOLDIER
TODAY ●	● GROWING ●	● MASTER
TOMORROW ●	● SURPRISED ●	● PUPPETEER
IMAGINATION ●	● BLOOMING ●	● TODDLER

METAPHOR MAKER

 **TOPIC**   is a / are    **MODIFIER**    **OBJECT**

_____

_____

_____

Explanation:

Examples:

Elaboration:

METAPHOR MAKER

Connect the dots to combine: a topic, a modifier and an object.
Make as many unique and meaningful combinations as you can.

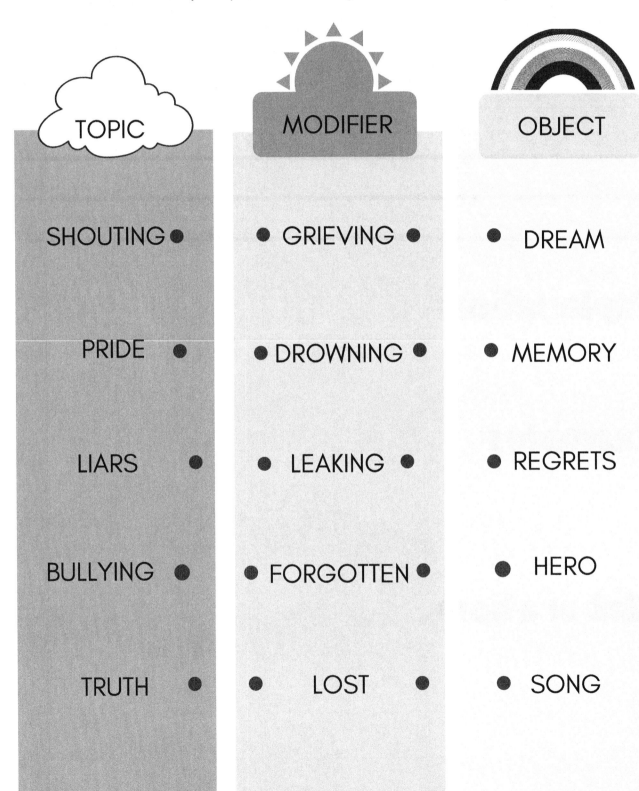

TOPIC	MODIFIER	OBJECT
SHOUTING	GRIEVING	DREAM
PRIDE	DROWNING	MEMORY
LIARS	LEAKING	REGRETS
BULLYING	FORGOTTEN	HERO
TRUTH	LOST	SONG

METAPHOR MAKER

 TOPIC **is a / are**  MODIFIER  OBJECT

_____

_____

_____

Explanation:

Examples:

Elaboration:

METAPHOR MAKER

Connect the dots to combine: a topic, a modifier and an object.
Make as many unique and meaningful combinations as you can.

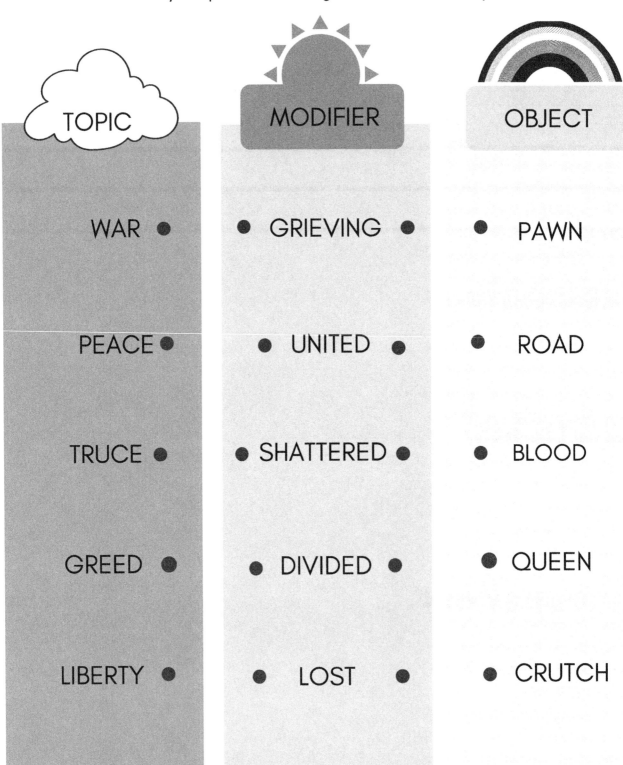

TOPIC	MODIFIER	OBJECT
WAR	GRIEVING	PAWN
PEACE	UNITED	ROAD
TRUCE	SHATTERED	BLOOD
GREED	DIVIDED	QUEEN
LIBERTY	LOST	CRUTCH

METAPHOR MAKER

 TOPIC | is a / are |  MODIFIER |  OBJECT

_____

_____

_____

Explanation:

Examples:

Elaboration:

METAPHOR MAKER

Connect the dots to combine: a topic, a modifier and an object.
Make as many unique and meaningful combinations as you can.

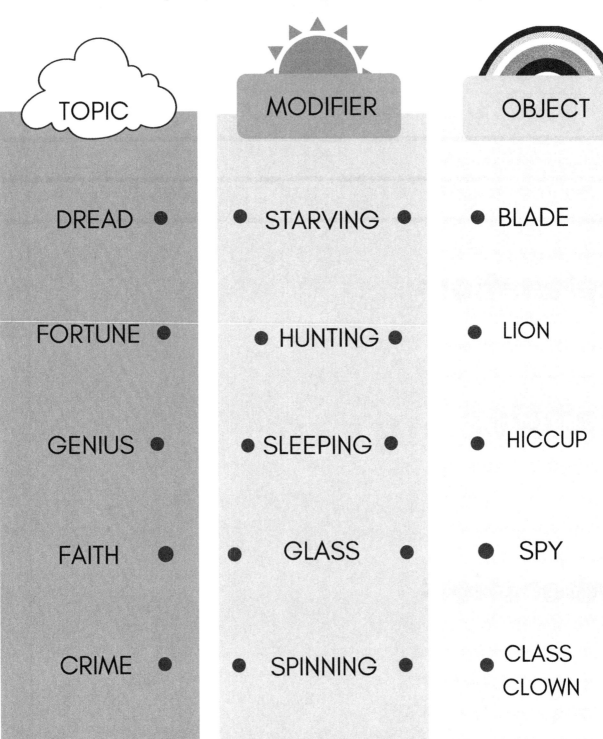

TOPIC	MODIFIER	OBJECT
DREAD	STARVING	BLADE
FORTUNE	HUNTING	LION
GENIUS	SLEEPING	HICCUP
FAITH	GLASS	SPY
CRIME	SPINNING	CLASS CLOWN

METAPHOR MAKER

 **TOPIC** ___is a___ / ___are___  MODIFIER  OBJECT

_____

_____

_____

Explanation:

Examples:

Elaboration:

METAPHOR MAKER

Connect the dots to combine: a topic, a modifier and an object.
Make as many unique and meaningful combinations as you can.

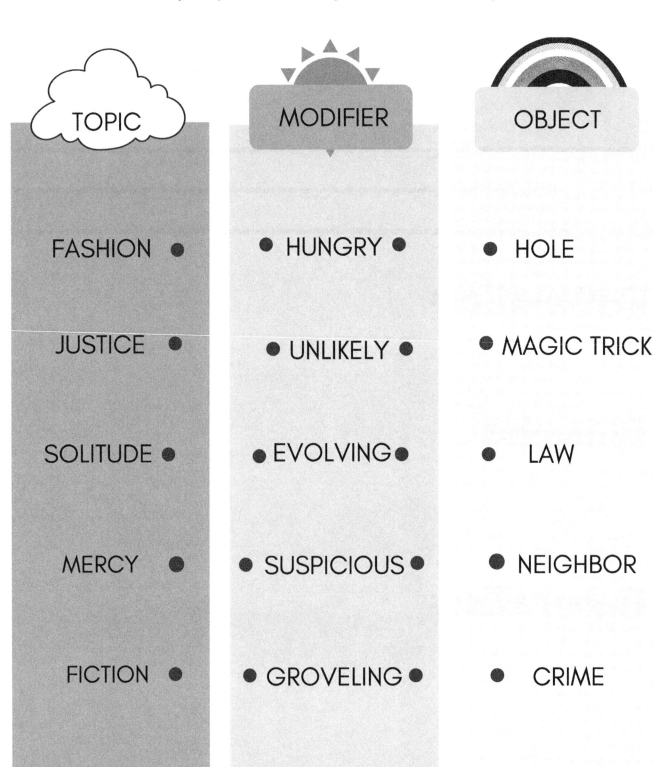

TOPIC	MODIFIER	OBJECT
FASHION	HUNGRY	HOLE
JUSTICE	UNLIKELY	MAGIC TRICK
SOLITUDE	EVOLVING	LAW
MERCY	SUSPICIOUS	NEIGHBOR
FICTION	GROVELING	CRIME

METAPHOR MAKER

 TOPIC is a / are  MODIFIER  OBJECT

_____

_____

_____

Explanation:

Examples:

Elaboration:

METAPHOR MAKER

Connect the dots to combine: a topic, a modifier and an object.
Make as many unique and meaningful combinations as you can.

TOPIC	MODIFIER	OBJECT
OMEN	ABANDONED	TRUMPET
DISAPPOINTMENT	FAKE	STETHOSCOPE
PAIN	BOLD	FARM
SUSPENCE	COLD	DOLL
HOPELESSNESS	PLASTIC	MEDAL

METAPHOR MAKER

 TOPIC | is a / are |  MODIFIER |  OBJECT

_____

_____

_____

Explanation:

Examples:

Elaboration:

METAPHOR MAKER

Connect the dots to combine: a topic, a modifier and an object.
Make as many unique and meaningful combinations as you can.

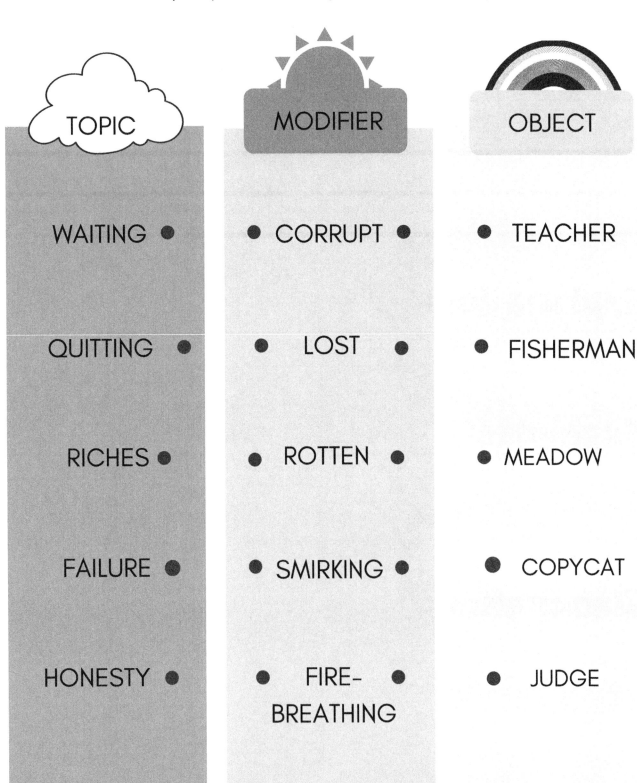

TOPIC	MODIFIER	OBJECT
WAITING	CORRUPT	TEACHER
QUITTING	LOST	FISHERMAN
RICHES	ROTTEN	MEADOW
FAILURE	SMIRKING	COPYCAT
HONESTY	FIRE-BREATHING	JUDGE

METAPHOR MAKER

 TOPIC   is a / are    MODIFIER    OBJECT

_____

_____

_____

Explanation:

Examples:

Elaboration:

METAPHOR MAKER

Connect the dots to combine: a topic, a modifier and an object.

Make as many unique and meaningful combinations as you can.

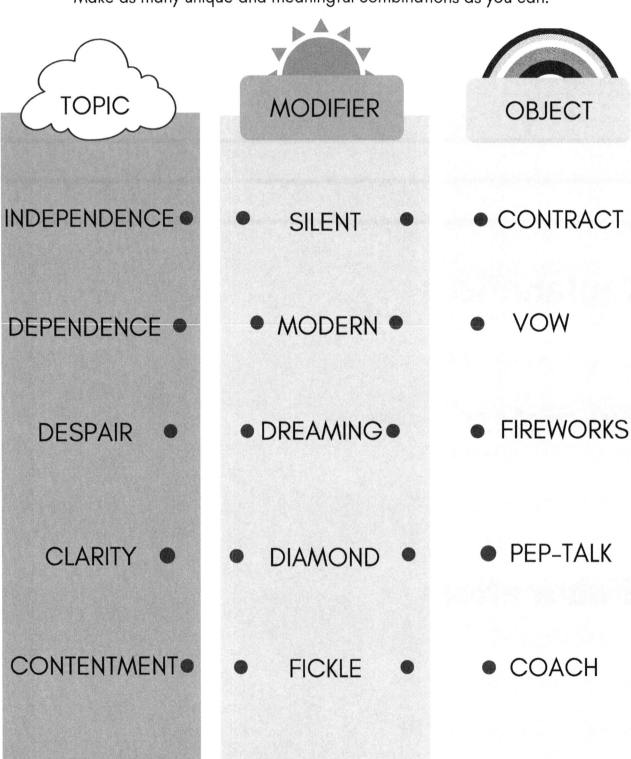

TOPIC	MODIFIER	OBJECT
INDEPENDENCE	SILENT	CONTRACT
DEPENDENCE	MODERN	VOW
DESPAIR	DREAMING	FIREWORKS
CLARITY	DIAMOND	PEP-TALK
CONTENTMENT	FICKLE	COACH

METAPHOR MAKER

 TOPIC   is a
                              ___
                              are    MODIFIER    OBJECT

_____

_____

_____

Explanation:

Examples:

Elaboration:

METAPHOR MAKER

Connect the dots to combine: a topic, a modifier and an object.
Make as many unique and meaningful combinations as you can.

TOPIC

MODIFIER

OBJECT

TOPIC	MODIFIER	OBJECT
INFAMY	DEAD	SMOKE
MISFORTUNE	BEATING	SEA
DESTINY	FLOATING	PEARL
STARDOM	GLITTERING	MOON
REPUTATION	FIGHTING	STAR

METAPHOR MAKER

TOPIC

is a
are

MODIFIER

OBJECT

_____

_____

_____

Explanation:

Examples:

Elaboration:

METAPHOR MAKER

Connect the dots to combine: a topic, a modifier and an object.
Make as many unique and meaningful combinations as you can.

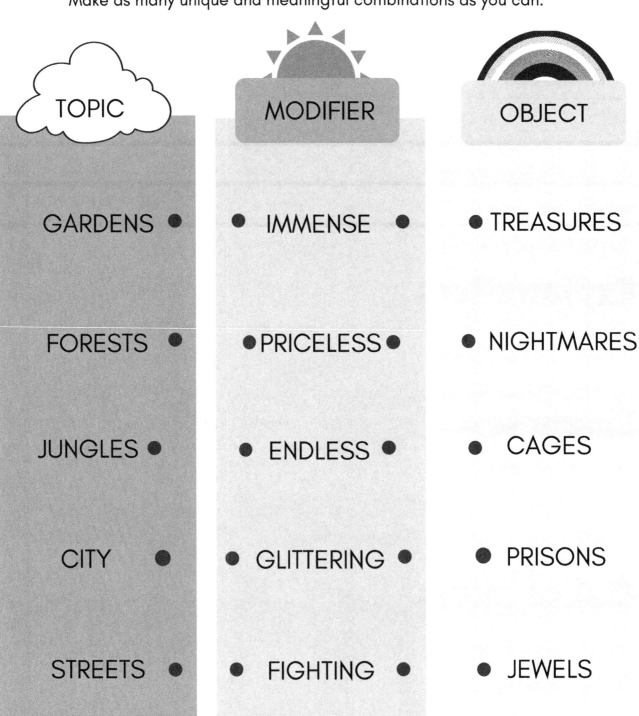

TOPIC	MODIFIER	OBJECT
GARDENS	IMMENSE	TREASURES
FORESTS	PRICELESS	NIGHTMARES
JUNGLES	ENDLESS	CAGES
CITY	GLITTERING	PRISONS
STREETS	FIGHTING	JEWELS

METAPHOR MAKER

 TOPIC | is a / are |  MODIFIER |  OBJECT

_____

_____

_____

Explanation:

Examples:

Elaboration:

METAPHOR MAKER

Connect the dots to combine: a topic, a modifier and an object.
Make as many unique and meaningful combinations as you can.

 **TOPIC**

 **MODIFIER**

 **OBJECT**

TOPIC	MODIFIER	OBJECT
TEENAGERS	NOVICE	ESCAPE ARTISTS
BABIES	OPTIMISTIC	ILLUSIONISTS
ADULTS	SHADY	WIZARDS
BABYSITTERS	EXASPERATED	WARDENS
CHILDREN	UNTRAINED	CONDUCTORS

METAPHOR MAKER

 TOPIC | is a / are |  MODIFIER |  OBJECT

_____

_____

_____

Explanation:

Examples:

Elaboration:

LET THE CARDS DECIDE

1. CUT OUT THE TOPIC, MODIFIER AND OBJECT CARDS
AT THE BACK OF THIS BOOK.
(BLANK CARDS ARE INCLUDED FOR YOU TO ADD NEW
VOCABULARY).

2. COMBINE TOPICS WITH MODIFIERS AND OBJECT CARDS TO
CREATE MORE METAPHORS.

3. DRAW CARDS RANDOMLY OR PURPOSELY
THE CARDS ARE **DOUBLE SIDED**,
SO BE SURE TO CONSIDER BOTH SIDES.

4. WRITE THE WORDS OR PASTE THE CARDS
ONTO THE SPACE PROVIDED.

5. HAVE FUN TAKING THE METAPHORS TO NEW PLACES.

MAKE MORE METAPHORS

POETRY **IS A** FRESH STORM

POETRY IS A
FRESH STORM

STORMS **ARE** LOST WORDS

STORMS ARE
LOST WORDS

LOST **IS** NEW INSPIRATION

LOST IS WHERE
INSPIRATION LIVES

INSPIRATION **IS A** NEW WELCOME MAT

INSPIRATION IS A NEW
WELCOME MAT

WAITING **IS A** HAPPY HOME

WAITING FOR YOU
TO COME HOME

EPIPHANY **IS AN** UNEXPECTED GUEST

WHERE EPIPHANIES
ARE UNEXPECTED
GUEST

USE THE CARDS AT THE BACK OF THE BOOK TO HELP YOU.

MAKE MORE METAPHORS

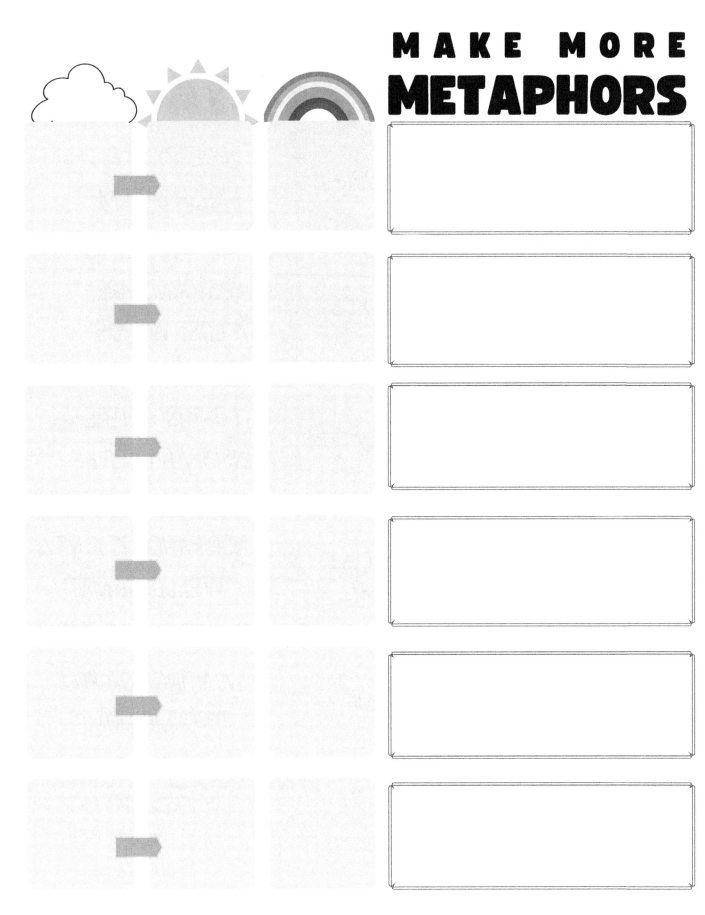

USE THE CARDS AT THE BACK OF THE BOOK TO HELP YOU.

EXPLANATIONS-EXAMPLES-ELABORATIONS

MAKE MORE METAPHORS

USE THE CARDS AT THE BACK OF THE BOOK TO HELP YOU.

EXPLANATIONS-EXAMPLES-ELABORATIONS

MAKE MORE METAPHORS

USE THE CARDS AT THE BACK TO HELP YOU.

EXPLANATIONS-EXAMPLES-ELABORATIONS

MAKE MORE
METAPHORS

USE THE CARDS AT THE BACK OF THE BOOK TO HELP YOU.

EXPLANATIONS-EXAMPLES-ELABORATIONS

MAKE MORE METAPHORS

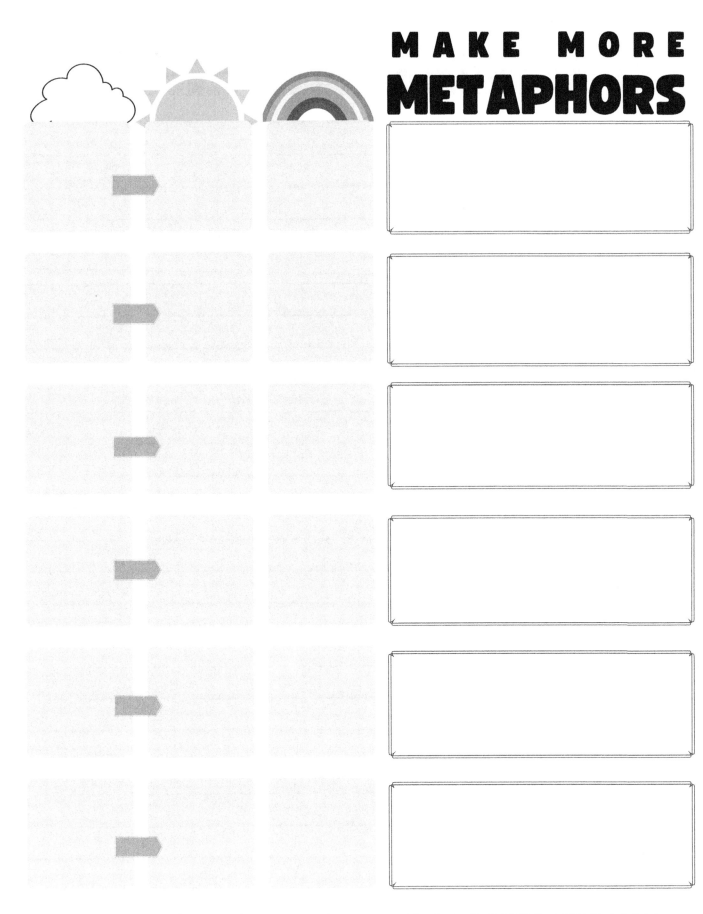

USE THE CARDS AT THE BACK OF THE BOOK TO HELP YOU.

EXPLANATIONS-EXAMPLES-ELABORATIONS

MAKE MORE METAPHORS

USE THE CARDS AT THE BACK OF THE BOOK TO HELP YOU.

EXPLANATIONS-EXAMPLES-ELABORATIONS

MAKE MORE METAPHORS

USE THE CARDS AT THE BACK OF THE BOOK TO HELP YOU.

EXPLANATIONS-EXAMPLES-ELABORATIONS

MAKE MORE
METAPHORS

USE THE CARDS AT THE BACK OF THE BOOK TO HELP YOU.

EXPLANATIONS-EXAMPLES-ELABORATIONS

MAKE MORE METAPHORS

USE THE CARDS AT THE BACK OF THE BOOK TO HELP YOU.

EXPLANATIONS-EXAMPLES-ELABORATIONS

MAKE MORE METAPHORS

USE THE CARDS AT THE BACK OF THE BOOK TO HELP YOU.

EXPLANATIONS-EXAMPLES-ELABORATIONS

MAKE MORE METAPHORS

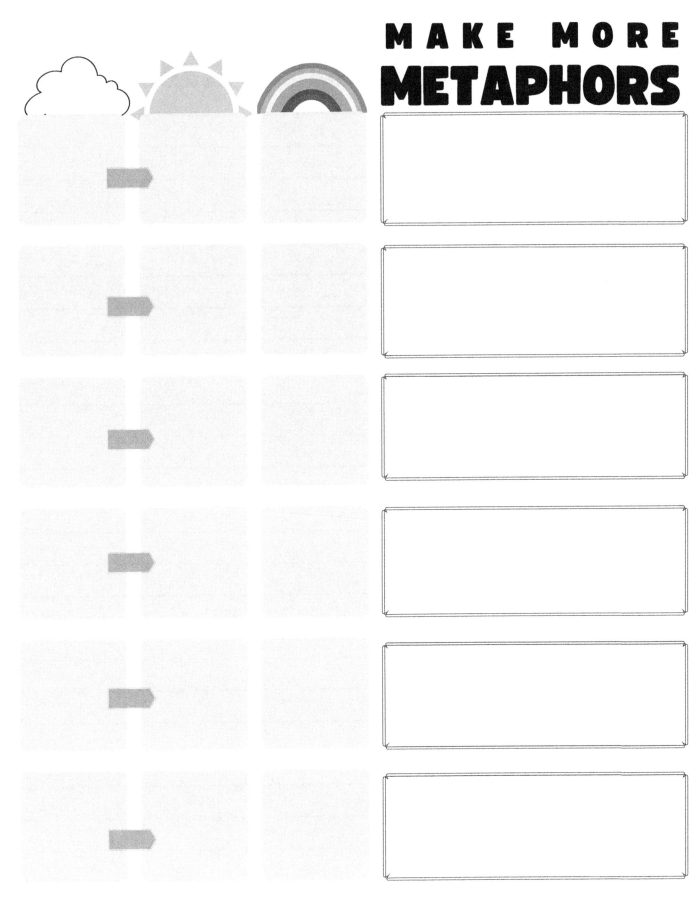

USE THE CARDS AT THE BACK OF THE BOOK TO HELP YOU.

EXPLANATIONS-EXAMPLES-ELABORATIONS

MAKE MORE
METAPHORS

USE THE CARDS AT THE BACK OF THE BOOK TO HELP YOU.

EXPLANATIONS-EXAMPLES-ELABORATIONS

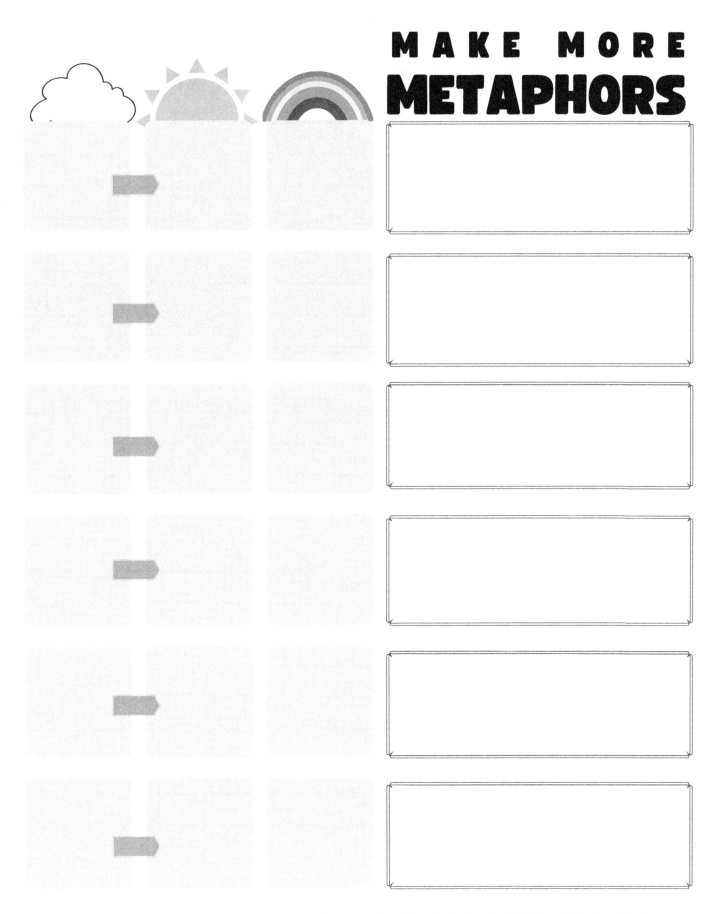

MAKE MORE METAPHORS

USE THE CARDS AT THE BACK OF THE BOOK TO HELP YOU.

EXPLANATIONS-EXAMPLES-ELABORATIONS

MAKE MORE METAPHORS

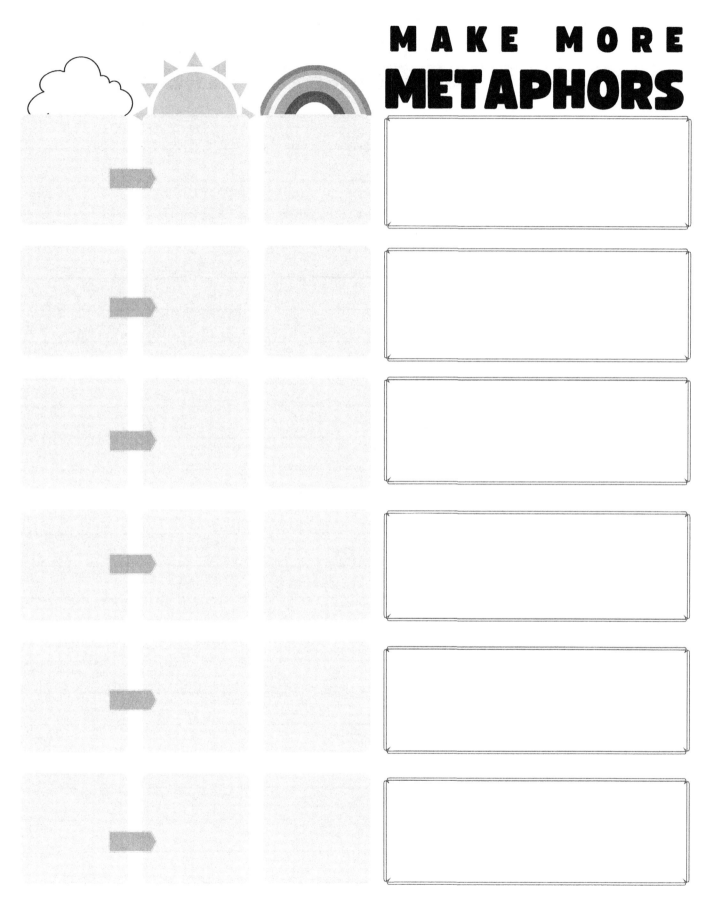

USE THE CARDS AT THE BACK OF THE BOOK TO HELP YOU.

EXPLANATIONS-EXAMPLES-ELABORATIONS

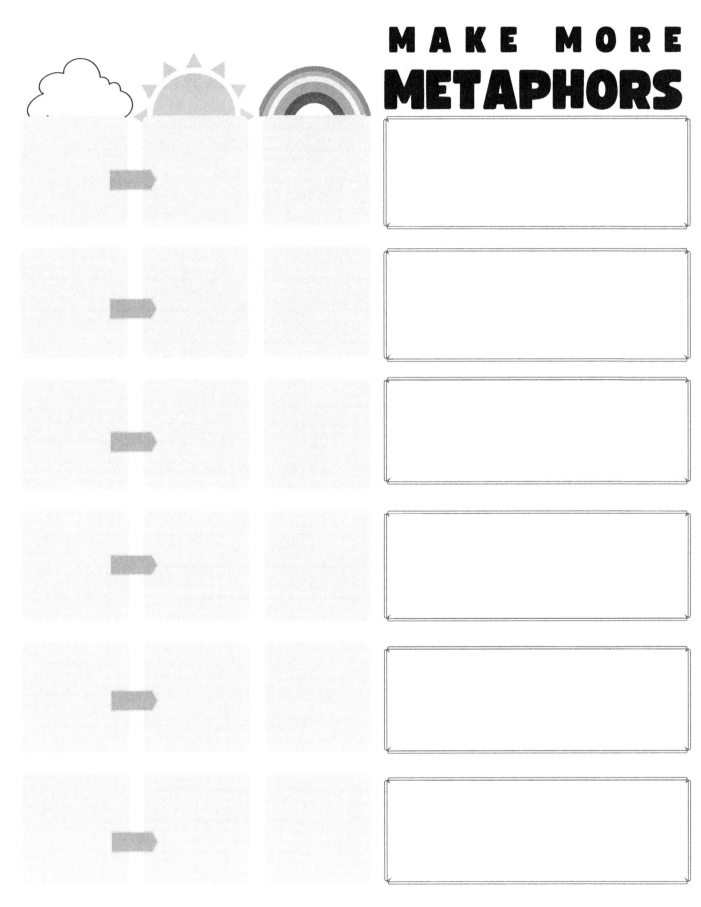

MAKE MORE METAPHORS

USE THE CARDS AT THE BACK OF THE BOOK TO HELP YOU.

EXPLANATIONS-EXAMPLES-ELABORATIONS

CUT OUT THE TOPIC, MODIFIER & OBJECT CARDS:

Mix & match to MAKE MORE METAPHORS

TOPIC CARDS: CUT OUT AND COMBINE WITH MODIFIERS AND OBJECT CARDS TO CREATE MORE METAPHORS

LOVE	TIME	HEART
POWER	HISTORY	FAMILY
TRUTH	MOTHER	FATHER
SOUL	MIND	BODY
LOSS	VICTORY	BEAUTY

topic cards: cut out and combine

LIFE	SLEEP	DEATH
LUCK	DAY	NIGHT
TRUST	PATIENCE	JEALOUSY
WISDOM	GRACE	ANGER
DEPRESSION	ANXIETY	HOPE

blank topic cards: Write your own, create, cut, and combine

blank topic cards: Write your own, create, cut, and combine

modifier cards: cut out and combine

FRESH	STALE	LOST
RELUCTANT	GENTLE	FOUND
SILENT	SECRET	BRIGHT
MAD	WILD	DIM
VACANT	BROKEN	IMPOSSIBLE

modifier cards: cut out and combine

BACKWARD	DIVIDED	DESPERATE
NEW	WET	CAREFUL
BOLD	DOWNHILL	TANGLED
DESERTED	UPHILL	DENSE
EXPLODING	BROKEN	SPARSE

modifier cards: cut out and combine

ILL-FATED	BACK-HANDED	FLOWING
CRUMBLING	JUGGLING	FLYING
DYING	TAME	PUFFED-UP
FLUFFY	FROZEN	FLAILING
LAUGHING	WILLFUL	INSANE

modifier cards: cut out and combine

CHILDISH	WICKED	FIGHTING
DANCING	SPEEDING	SULLEN
SLOW	CRAWLING	GROWLING
SHARP	WISHING	SWEATING
ANCIENT	MISCHIEVOUS	DEADLY

blank modifier cards: WRITE YOUR OWN, cut out, and combine

blank modifier cards: WRITE YOUR OWN, cut out, and combine

object cards: cut out and combine

MIRROR	MASK	STORM
MOUNTAIN	CLOUD	RAINBOW
TREE	BIRD	SONG
JUNGLE	STREAM	ANIMAL
HERO	WATERFALL	OCEAN

object cards: cut out and combine

WHALE	CHICKEN	SNOWMAN
KITE	TIARA	BLESSING
KISS	HUG	CURSE
KNIFE	BEAST	WALL
BATTLE	VOW	ZOO

object cards: cut out and combine

VIOLIN	VALENTINE	CANDY
BASKET	SNOW	SOCK
CANDLE	GLOVE	SHOE
BRICK	DOG	PREY
PREDATOR	DOOR	WINDOW

object cards: cut out and combine

POOL	NURSERY	MARKET
LUNCH	BRUNCH	BREAKFAST
PENCIL	PEN	BOOT
BASEBALL BAT	HOCKEY PUCK	MAGICIAN
NET	GOAL	HORN

blank object cards: WRITE your own, cut out, and combine

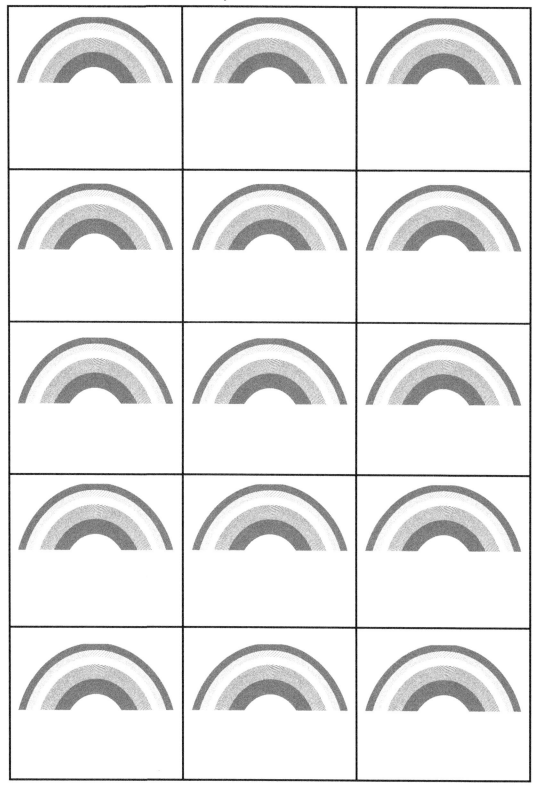

blank object cards: WRITE your own, cut out, and combine

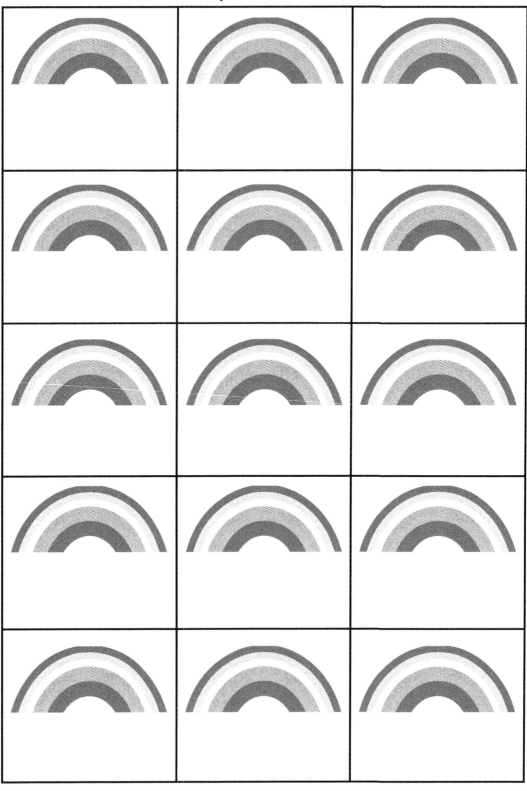

MORE ABOUT METAPHORS...

Metaphors come in other forms.

Play around with analogies and say something
no one has ever said before.
As long as you imply that your topic **is** something
that it literally **isn't**, you are being metaphorical.
For example:

A fresh storm of poetry arrived without warning.
It rained rhymes all night long,
and today, we are all swimming in a sea
of poems.

NOW, GO PLAY WITH YOU WORDS!

MORE ABOUT EXPLANATIONS, EXAMPLES AND ELABORATIONS....

Brainstorm vocabulary and create word banks. You may even wish to do a bit of research to gather vocabulary. Wikipedia can be a great place to gather vocabulary on nearly any topic or object.

Poetry

rhyme
words
meter
line-break
metaphors
similes
hyperbole
personification
love

Storm

rain
wind
torrential
wind
hurricane
umbrella
flood
pitter-patter
pouring
hail

*Use your word bank to help you explain,
give examples and elaborate on your topic.*

Have fun!

Jules Horne Dramatic Techniques

Printed in Great Britain
by Amazon

38428727R00057